YOU'RE LOOK FINE

Imran

ISBN 978-93-5610-617-8
© Imran 2022
Published in India 2022 by Pencil

A brand of
One Point Six Technologies Pvt. Ltd.
123, Building J2, Shram Seva Premises,
Wadala Truck Terminal, Wadala (E)
Mumbai 400037, Maharashtra, INDIA
E connect@thepencilapp.com
W www.thepencilapp.com

DISCLAIMER: *The opinions expressed in this book are those of the authors and do not purport to reflect the views of the Publisher.*

Author biography

Oh I'm thinking of changing my mind
All I really need right now
Is plenty of sunshine
One more chance to prove

CONTENTS

I Am Doing The Dishes

I am doing the dishes
I am like a star I am flashing
Gotta get my feet on the ground
When the world's turned around
I am like a star
I am doing the dishes
I am running the home test
Then I am like a star
I am doing the dishes
I am running the home test
And I am like a star, yeah
And I am like a star
I am looking out for the rest of me
I am never alone, never alone
I am never alone
I am never alone, never alone
I am gonna get there girl
I am a long long time
I am a long long time
I am a long long time..

I Love this Guitar

I love this guitar
You're so close I'll be yours
And it's so easy, just take this guitar
Crazy girl loves this guitar
So c'mon and on
Rock and roll angels, soft lights and sirens
Just ringing through the air
Hear the union hall of worship
I got a guitar ohh
I love this guitar
I love this guitar
I love this guitar
I love this guitar
I love this guitar baby
In your cold and buried mind

I'm Going Insane

I'm Going Insane
With your eyes to burn,
As good as you can be.
And you can look in the
eyes of every guy in the band
But that would cost you,
You got to take your pay cheque
and you got to try and make it
back aliveAnd you can try to take
your money and you got to do that
what you mean to meYou can try
for the big time,
Try to get you to stay.
Well I need you girl to drive me crazy
I'm lost in this town,
It's a comin' townI gotta find myself,
I need you girlI gotta take my love and tear it apart
So I can start againI'm going insaneYes I'm going crazy

Strange

It's strange how you are
totally different from what
you were some months ago,
when we met,
And I couldn't tell if
this is how you are,
Or I lost the real you?
I wish I could have you back.

So when I say I've loved you,
It doesn't mean I no more love you,
But I mean I still love the
person you were before,
And I couldn't love the new you now
Everytime I'm with you,
I miss the old you even more!

Well

"...it's the thought that counts..."
Well, I've thought about forgiving
them for long and have pushed
away the thoughts of revenge!

Oh

O poor delicate soul of mine,
How do you try to fit in this world?
Where people have no heart,
Where People tend to betray others.

You think no one is bad?
You think people have reasons,
To be the cruelest version of themselves?

At least

In the last, of the last moment of my life.
My mind was searching, a piece of paper to write.

It is this unfinished poem,
that kept on knocking at my door,
all this time.
Now there it greets me,
on the other side in the heaven,
with a smile.

At last, it was death.
My poem's concluding line.

Overpass

Was it by design, that we drifted a few books apart, and drew each other too, on the blank pages we had left just to give ourselves enough space to breathe?

I've grown more thirst than I have the wine to clear my throat, for all the beautiful things that lay unsaid in pages printed in this dark, fuzzy cursive.

Was it by design, that I found you in the middle of the story, standing clear in the way of faint faded sentences, and you glanced back at me like the star that had always been waiting to sparkle when the night comes?

Was it by design, or was it by TRAGEDY, that a few phonemes later I couldn't see you again, when you'd faded, like the rest of the pages, until all there was to look at, and feel, was nothing, but the nostalgic smell of wood, and it all became a perfect fairytale?

Or was it just another random event, amongst all the things in the sky that were yet to happen, whose complexities we will both never discern, except to just stare, and listen, to other useless things and ignore this, that has become of us?

It is not

Many would think, her tongue is mute;
it is not.
It is for intimate murmur,
affectionate whisper, midnight lullaby.
Her timid, little voice is there to accompany the silence.

Love is composed of a single soul
inhabiting two bodies.

Something

There was something about him that threw
sane thinking out the window and just put
rationality to its knees.

Something in the way he spoke that kindled a
forbidden fire and woke a sleeping dragon.

When the sun receeded back keepingsix
her light away, when the clock stroke six,
I would shed what made me me and
approach him free of doubts and all reason.

Over Again

Tell me how the world broke you,
how it shattered your soul to parts,
how the wind blew them away.

How the darkness played you a whole
orchestra as the moonlight slept in your eyes.

Tell me, even though you don't need to.
Because I know how your tears would
sound like, I cried them before.

I know how a Lily like you would
wither over and over again.

Still, tell me, because you're the only one
who I wouldn't mind to listen to over
and over again.
My dear younger sister.

You

Smiling to keep myself,
A part of the world,
Where I had to hide myself,
Hiding the pain,
And smiling through tears,
Masking my fears.

Where's the real me?
Where's the real me,
You, you
You were there to help me get it back,
Untrue, untrue,
You were the one to hurt me.

You built me,
And then let me fall,
I was injured before,
But never had it hurt this badly.

Being with you made me realise,
How weak I had been
This entire time,
How I hated myself,
Hated myself for who I was,
For what the world did,

You, you made me realise,
How it feels to love myself,
How it feels to smile, to live,
To know myself,
But did i deserve it,
Not what the world did,
But what you did?

You made me realise,
I didn't deserve hatred,
Told me I'll be loved,
I hoped it was you,
You mended my broken self,
Now that you broke it,
Who'll help me mend it?

Trying to make it

Alone but not Lonely
Isolating myself from city lights,
To talk to my soul under the stars,
To hear it's tale of how it's been hurt,
How it healed and to adore it's scars.

I try to recognise my soul,
Hidden behind my anger, smile and pain,
Or disguised within the words,
I speak , write or hide.
Thus, being to myself
Doesn't really go in vain.

Now I know myself as a person I love
And don't need to impress others,
As I've known my soul in black,
And need not to show them
In different colours.

Let me

I'm drawn away from the world.
Locked under the weight of my pain.

Unhinged by the loneliness.
Unsettled by its uncertainty.

Such is a mess I've become.
All that I could be, is all that I hate.

I don't miss people.
Though my heart is still beating.

I'm drawn away from myself.
Locked and forgotten by the world.

So please,
let me put an end to my sorrows.

Let me settle,
Let my death be in vain.

You call yourself villain

"You call yourself villain,
yet you dare praise our Lord as
if you're one of the good men?"

"I praise Him, because he is the
almighty master of both good and bad.
If you don't realise this, perhaps you
should contemplate more on your blind faith."

It's just neh

They are the scars from wars,
From the the internal battle of you and them,
They reflect the pain,
They symbolise your bravery.
Your tears don't make you weak,
They show that you've been strong for too long.
Your silence isn't cowardice,
It's just you giving yourself some time.
So be proud of those scars,
They show that you've won many wars.

Your fear doesn't make you weak,
It's a sign of you dealing with abuse.
Your shaky hands don't make you powerless,
They just show so how much you've been suppressed.
You are injured body doesn't make it beautiful any less,
Those bruises just show how bad they were,
It's not you, it's their sick minds,
Your scars, your pain,
Just proves that right.

So believe in yourself,
You are strong,
It's them in the wrong,
Your scars make you strong,

And your pain shows your worth,
Don't let it get to you,
Because in the end,
You're the survivor,
Who came out much, more stronger.

Closed your eyes

"Your hands are cold," She said,
holding my hands in hers to warm
them up a bit.

"Aren't they always, though,"
was what I wanted to say.

But the way she held my hands,
the soft smile on her face, eyes
closed as if warming up my hands
was the only thing she wanted to
focus on, seemed as if she held the air
of a mother. This petite girl,
seemed to take the role of a caretaker,
a guardian.

I felt the serenity in her air melt my
sarcastic, bitter tone, leaving a ghost
of peace sleeping on my lips.

Thus, I closed my eyes as well,
listening to her silence.

Walk Away

Take time.
Walk away, Disappear.
And when you come back later,
You will handle it better.

These walls that are surrounding,
This cage that is rattling,
Are your creations.
Free yourself, for you deserve it.
Whatever is left of your sanity, preserve it.

Severe off all ties. One thread at a time.
Do not think too much into the future.
Your present needs you.
The future can be built,
When your today is in place.

You worry a lot.
And about what!
Time was never yours to begin with,
And you will never be able to mould it,
It is okay to bend. Relax a little, let go.

Accept that failure.
It did not work out.

Accepting it will do wonders.
This precariousness needs no further effort,
Let it hang, for as long as it may.

Live leisurely.
What you truly need,
Is you, yourself.
If you cannot fulfill your own void,
Then you are no good for anyone else.

Make no conscious efforts to improve,
Life should be a smooth ride.
Whatever you needed to know, you do.
You float. You glide.
When you do not care, things abide.

Lily

I was in awe of the wreath of dark curled smoke slipping down your tongue spilling on the marble floors I made at the sullen dawn,
I was marveling at the marine blue pool of hot water tumbling down the valley of your neck and disappearing through the mountains as the twilight sun,

I was lost amid the lands of crimson rinsed bow of your tempting lip lowering like the forlorn moon,
I was bewitched by the doll face sprinkled by the silver to utter perfection,
I was held captive between the crooks and curves of the emerald silk knitted to a stunning gown.

I've Read it all

I've read it all,
The lies of your eyes,
The truth that you hide,
Your fake smile,
The emotions you couldn't confide,
The stories of the nights you cried,
All your futile tries,
The secrets you left behind.

I've known you more than
You think I do.
Maybe that's why you still
choose to lie..

You and I bleed

You bleed, I bleed.
Outside you,
Life's never had
A clear print.
You giggle, I chuckle.
And I can't be there,
Where you're not.
Instead, you're written
All over dark spaces,
In light font it's clear
To see, I'm fond of you.
Whisper me away,
And I'll dance right
Back at your tongue.

Everyone

Everyone believe in them—because of that stupid prophecy. They thought at first their master was the same. He was assigned to train them to fight against what calamity was to come—or rather, the greater calamity to come. They never wanted to do this. They wasn't a fighter, ever only dreamed of a quiet life. Surely people had been mistaken?

But they knew the master. If there anything they learned about that man these last months they trained under him it was that he was a man with proper head over his shoulders. He wouldn't be a "master" otherwise. So they knew, when he said he believed in them, it wasn't because of that vague prophecy.

So now, laying in their bed, glaring up on the ceiling, they questioned themselves; would they also believe him?

It just neh

As my reflection stared back at me,
I feel conflicted yet again,
Looking at the smile,
Which never dimmed even a bit,
And the colours which faded away each passing day,
The thought of living without my other half too scary,
Has been a reality for past unfortunate years,
As I stare longer, I zone out yet again,
To a world, where it was just the two of us,
With our hands intertwined, and faces wide with smiles,
As I reach out my hands, to capture the moment,
It runs away, afraid
Leaving me alone with my thoughts,
And you, smiling just the same,
I wonder if that smile will remain,
When I come to you as well,
For it had always been reserved for me,
As the fresh tears stream down,
And I reveal the feel of you in my arms,
I can't help but wish to meet you,
Just for a moment,
For I know, life is cruel
And it will make me suffer again.
I look down at your face,
Held in my wrinkled hands,

It's been years, yet your absence feels just the same,
But I know better than to hurry to meet you,
For we once promised,
To never let go of life, until death calls our names.

On the brink of horizon

On the brink of horizon
My sun sets with you,
On the sentence of anguish
My agony lies next to you.

With every bargain
That I make for
My fragile feelings,
With your cold currency;
I somehow question myself
Of even having the love anymore.

Remember

I am trying to remember
The times of our silence
where I felt the cold of your embrace
Or times of where you make me feel vain
because all beneath that is hard to let go
when your soulmate is traveler, that you cant get a hold

A sedentary heart, seeking for settling
falls in love with a wonder soul
like a wind that blows

A beauty I never knew exist
I saw it in your eyes, I felt it in your voice

And now all that is gone,
knowing that life can be more,
I feel dead while I'm living
going to breath like I was doing

These few moments of connection
were enough to change my ways
but time as it always does
puts me back to my old railway

Forgiveness

They say it's important to forgive for you to heal and move on. That it's important to forgive for your own happiness. They also suggest you to forgive but never to forget. This makes me wonder. How can you hypnotise yourself to forget the hurt and the pain you might have gone through. Time heals the wounds but then there are certain wounds which leave a scar forever. You feel you are healed and have moved on from the past trauma. You feel you are the epitome of strength. When suddenly, Lo!!! There's a reflection from the past which comes to haunt you. The reflection wants only one thing- Your complete forgiveness. And now, you have no other option but to forgive. The years of ranting and bickering stops suddenly, and all the hatred gets turned into forgiveness, prayers and best wishes for that soul. Feelings can be deceitful and atrocious at the same time. You never know what point they can trigger for you and when all your strength can start faltering. But then, your mind reminds you ' You have already fought so many battles before, you can't give up now' You stand up again and fight back to become stronger, wiser and a better person. Forgiveness is the virtue of the strong people after all!

Griff

"True beauty, the kind that doesn't fade or wash off, takes time. It takes incredible endurance. It is the slow drip that creates the stalactite, the shaking of the Earth that creates mountains, the constant pounding of the waves that breaks up the rocks and smooths the rough edges. And from the violence, the furor, the raging of the winds, the roaring of the waters, something better emerges, something that would have otherwise never existed.

And so we endure. We have faith that there is purpose. We hope for things we can't see. We believe there are lessons in loss, power in love, and that we have within us the potential for a beauty so magnificent, our bodies can't contain it.

Trust

Trust your dreams enough to pursue them.

Abandon the false notion that you are not good enough. Move and do that thing; you will see you were misleading yourself that you weren't good enough. You are a possibility.

Stay motivated to keep at it. Challenges don't mean impossible, it means "in-process".

Achievement is the goal, but self-improvement is the mark of success. It is what you become along the road to achievement that makes you a success.

Make friends with the right people. Avoid snakes and foxes, it is in their nature to be vile and cunning.

Protect your Soul. If someone is giving you another identity, that is when the soul is negotiated to be bought.

Me

Yes it's another break of dawn to see your beautiful face
again.
I wonder what it was that made me fall helplessly in love
with you.
Your smile alone brightens up my day, the thought of you
illuminates my face.
We have been best of friends since childhood
But you never give me that Charming smile you always
give those random girls.
I've hidden my crush from you for three years, and today I
believe it's the most perfect day to tell you how I feel.
With the birds singing in the summer break.
And a trip we planned the day before to the beach.
Today can't be any less perfect, my heart keeps missing it's
beat in joy.
Finally my crush will be mine I thought.
For last night while we lay drunk on your bed.
You told me how beautiful I am, and I lay on your chest
while sleep got the better of me.
There you are my Prince charming, my heart skips a beat
when I see you.
I've got to put it under control I thought.
The sun kissed his face as he jogged down to the beach.
I memorized my lines one more time lest fumble.
And then I saw her looking up at you and giving you the

cutest smile ever.

You came close and said "Hi Josie meet my girlfriend Amy".

My heart lost it's beat as I realized you'll never be mine.

I watched helplessly as you smile and kissed her....my heart turned cold as I watched you do what you always do,"Throw me aside".

A quote

A quote attributed to Viktor Frankl says, "What is to give light must endure burning".

Another way to look at this is that those with a call on their lives will suffer a great of affliction. The path through the dark system of this world is not an easy one. Known and unknown enemies will make a sport of you from here and there.

Sometimes I get tired wanting to be the good guy, to help people, to teach and communicate glad tidings. Sometimes, I don't want to write anything that increases consciousness or that makes people better.

Sometimes, I want to play the devil, to revenge, to avenge, to be ruthless, because I cannot understand why this pain has to be suffered, why I should be one lone guy in a field of ravenous wolves and cunning foxes who are skilled at masking their intentions and crafting your end while also pretending to be your guides and mentors.

Then, you see it another way that this burning of your experience is the necessary trial that you must face, the demons that you must battle, the initiation that must see you emerge into your shine.

Even at this realisation, there is no consolation, no guarantee that after the burning, you will shine. Many are gone who left the scenes of the battle of life as nobodies. They got burnt.

Written by Victor Negro.

On a big ugly long thin fall

On A Big Ugly Long Thin FallIt's funny, I'm not saying goodbye, whoa, we've all got to walk the road where you goDon't you think the snow just looks like springWhen you want to smell the roses and not think about meAnd the snow is just a big ugly long thin fallOn a big ugly long thin fallAnd the only time that I hear that I want a new life is when your hands are like papercut paperThen a voice is just for me and you're the only face I seeThere's a time for a new leaf to growAnd a time for a time to be freeAnd a time to find a new face and another skin to blendI said the only time that I hear that I want a new life is when your hands are like papercut paper